Under the Gaze of God

Blessed Edward Johannes Maria Poppe
(1890–1924)
Beatified October 3, 1999

Under the Gaze of God

Counsels for Perfection
&
Sparks

BLESSED EDWARD POPPE

Translated from the French by
C. M. COLOMBE

With a biographical sketch by
ISAAC J. OLSON

First published in Dutch as *Onder Gods Oog*
Translated into French as *Sous le regard de Dieu*
First published in English by
Arouca Press © 2020

All rights reserved. No part of this book
may be reproduced or transmitted, in any
form or by any means, without permission

ISBN: 978-1-989905-34-0

Arouca Press
PO Box 55003
Bridgeport PO
Waterloo, ON N2J3G0
Canada
www.aroucapress.com
Send inquiries to info@aroucapress.com

Book and cover design
by Michael Schrauzer
Cover photograph courtesy of
Fr. Lawrence Lew, O.P.

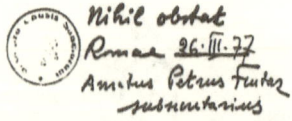

Nihil obstat
V. DESCAMPS
can., libr. cens.

Imprimatur
Tornaci, die 13 iulii 1967
J. Thomas, *vic. gen.*

TABLE OF CONTENTS

INTRODUCTION TO THE
   FRENCH EDITION xi

BIOGRAPHICAL SKETCH xv

COUNSELS FOR PERFECTION 1

  Carry your cross 3

  Spiritual reading 3

  Prayer and mortification 4

  Peace 5

  Gaudete in Domino,
     Rejoice in the Lord 6

  Serenity or haste? 7

  To love the Cross 9

  Charity is not weakness 9

  O Crux, ave. Hail, holy Cross 10

  Communia non communiter, Common
     things, uncommonly well 11

  Fidelity in little things 13

  Weak, but trusting 14

  Noli timere. Why be afraid? 15

  Confide, fili mi,
     Have confidence, my child 16

Willing is power! 16
"Today is the day of salvation". 17
"Lord, teach us to pray". 18
Ambula coram me et esto perfectus,
   Walk in my presence
   and be perfect 23
Ego sum panis vivus,
   I am the living bread 24
The kingdom of God is taken
   by force! 26
Esto mitis! Be meek! 27
Ave Maria 27
Be a martyr! 29
Break the bonds! 30
Guard your tongue! 31
Become a saint 31
Nihil sum et nescivi!,
   I am nothing and I do not know! . . 32
In cruce salus!,
   Salvation comes from the Cross . . . 35
Come and follow Me! 36
Tristis es anima mea . . .,
   My soul is filled with sorrow 37
Trial or chastisement? 39
Passions or the cross? 40

Table of Contents

"But Jesus was silent..." 40

For the hours of aridity 41

Obedience and humility 43

Ama nesciri!,
   Gladly be unknown! 46

St. Joseph 47

Trust and resignation. 48

Christo confixus sum cruci,
   Fixed to the cross with Christ. . . . 50

Do you fear the cross? 52

Felix culpa,
   Happy fault 52

Divine Providence 53

SPARKS 59

1. Sanctity & Perfection 61
2. The Eucharist. 71
3. Marian Devotion. 73
4. Faith & Trust. 83
5. Love 89
6. Religious Obedience 95
7. Poverty 99
8. *Ascesis*, Mortification,
    & Self-offering 101
9. Humility. 107

UNDER THE GAZE OF GOD

10. Love of the Cross & Trials 113
11. Prayer & Meditation. 123
12. The Apostolate 131

A PRAYER FOR BLESSED EDWARD
   POPPE'S CANONIZATION. 137

INTRODUCTION
to the French Edition (2015)

FR. MARTIAL LEKEUX, OFM

FATHER EDWARD POPPE, a holy Belgian priest, whose cause for canonization is under way, was an unparalleled master of the spiritual life. Like the Curé of Ars (whom he resembles in many points) and as with all genuine guides of souls, he first lived in his heroic life what he taught to others.

This booklet brings together some extracts from his numerous writings, some of which achieved impressive print runs. These thoughts, which have an incisive power and profound piety reminiscent of *The Imitation of Christ*, are of the kind which will do great good to souls who desire to draw closer to God.

BIOGRAPHICAL SKETCH

The *Counsels for Perfection* are pious reflections which, in a very simple way, Fr. Poppe wrote for his sister Eugenie, a Presentation Nun, who was his confidant. As is the rule for those whom God wants to sanctify, the worthy young lady was not without her difficulties in the convent; she had truly painful trials. She asked her brother to give her some advice for her spiritual life.

Vicar of a parish in Ghent at the time, Father Poppe was overwhelmed by his duties. It was not effortless for him, bit by bit, to compose these little meditations. Finally, on February 4, 1917, he wrote to his sister, "Your little collection is almost finished. For the most part, it is comprised of thoughts which have occupied me in my own spiritual life. It has often cost me to write a page, but I did not think this was time wasted. And it's a happy mortification for me, to which I gladly submit in the hope of pleasing you."

Introduction

Having been published in Flemish, these spiritual notes were copied by hand a hundred times by those who, having savored them, made them their preferred spiritual reading. Priests, religious, and laity will appreciate the supernatural wisdom, unction, and power of these reflections made "under the gaze of God."

The second part of the collection, *Sparks*, is composed of short sentences gleaned from Fr. Poppe's works and arranged under various headings according to their subject. They have already appeared separately in the Flemish review *De Stem uit Moerzeke* dedicated to Fr. Poppe. Many have made these spiritual maxims, cast like medals, their inseparable *vademecum*. They have found in these potent words guidance for their life, nourishment for their prayer, and, for their apostolate, original and luminous formulations.

The Flemish edition of this booklet has already reached thirty thousand copies.

BIOGRAPHICAL SKETCH

This shows how much this little book answers the needs of the faithful. French readers will find an equal benefit in coming into contact with his strong teaching, his penetrating piety, and the sanctifying power it exercises.

BIOGRAPHICAL SKETCH

ISAAC J. OLSON

THE LIFE AND WORK OF this beloved Belgian saint belongs to the vast family of saints and blesseds surrounding the Wounded and Sacred Heart of Jesus. Bl. Edward's motto was: "I would rather die than half-serve God," conveying how his spirituality was serious, masculine, and thoroughly evangelical. Edward Poppe, a simple parish priest, dedicated himself to the holy priesthood and offered himself to Christ as a victim for the sanctification of priests. When he died at the age of 33, he had planted the seeds which would affect the lives of priests in Belgium and across the world for years to come.

Edward Johannes Maria Poppe was born on December 18, 1890 in Temse, Belgium, to Désiré and Josefa. As the third child of eleven (and eldest son), Edward was meant to succeed his father in their baking business but at an early age he sensed the call to the priesthood, to which his parents gratefully consented. From his mother grew a natural sense for prayer and kindness, while from his father developed a manly strength and love for hard work. Edward learned theological life in the heart of his own family, where the prayers of the parents and their living charity endowed him with a special sensitivity for the poor and a deep sense of sacrifice, justice, and human dignity.

When Edward was nine years old, Pope Leo XIII issued the encyclical letter *Annum Sacrum*, in which he decreed that the entire human race be consecrated to the Most Sacred Heart of Jesus. This public consecration took place on June 11, 1899, spurred on by the request of Our Lord to Blessed Maria Droste Zu Vischering (Maria of the Divine Heart).

Biographical Sketch

On March 20, 1902, Edward made his First Holy Communion and received confirmation at the age of twelve. Four years later, Edward entered the St. Nicholas Minor Seminary in Waas. Upon commencing his formal journey to the priesthood, Edward's joy was unbounded and, as he wrote to his sister, he resolved to become a priest after the Heart of Jesus. Shortly after entering the minor seminary, his father died suddenly when Edward was just sixteen. While he considered it his duty as eldest son to carry on the family business, his father had made his mother uphold their promise to allow Edward to answer God's call to the priesthood.

Twice Edward was summoned to military service in the midst of World War I, interrupting his seminary studies and depriving him of regular reception of the Sacraments. Placed among faithless young men who subjected Edward to derision because he wanted to be a priest, he better understood the strength and courage Catholic men needed in the military, drawn from regular reception of the Eucharist and like-minded friendships. This experience prepared him for his later ministry as chaplain to Catholic seminarians and religious conscripted for their mandatory service. Finally, in 1915, Edward obtained an exemption from Cardinal Mercier, Bishop of Malines, to withdraw from active military duty and resume his seminary training.

As a seminarian, Edward was reminded that the priest is called to participate actively in the sufferings of Christ in a vocation of generous love and self-sacrificial abandonment. Consecrating himself to the Heart of Jesus, he accepted all that the will of God ordained for his life. Writing to his sister in religious life, he said: "Knowing that I will be crowned with thorns, that a spear will pierce my heart, that I will be hurt and humiliated both corporally and spiritually.... I will not give up my

Biographical Sketch

vocation, but I'm counting on your maternal help. Make me another Christ."

On May 1, 1916, Edward was ordained to the holy priesthood and consecrated his entire ministry to the Eucharistic Heart of Jesus as a victim soul for sinners so that, in the celebration of the Holy Sacrifice of the Mass, he would practice what the Angel of Fatima was requesting at nearly the same time. In the second apparition, the Angel of Fatima implored the children to "offer sacrifice to God in reparation for the sins by which He is offended, and in supplication for sinners."

Father Poppe knew that it was "by prayer, sacrifice, and Communion" that we can "bring the Divine Heart of Jesus to triumph over the world." This constant desire of his was in harmony with the growth in devotion to the Sacred Heart, a devotion which desires to love, honor, and console Our Lord in the Blessed Sacrament by the offering of one's life of prayer, penance, and charity.

He maintained these ideals of sacrifice and identification with Christ, the High Priest, throughout his short and inspiring life.

Father Poppe radiated a simple and modest interior, whereby his joy and empathy were revealed in a face full of intelligence and kindness. He loved living a simple and modest life, depriving himself of his possessions in order to aid the poor of his parish of St. Coleta, even to the extent of pawning his beloved violin to help a needy woman while her husband was imprisoned.

Writing to a brother priest, Father Poppe said: "Let us ourselves be examples and expect everything from the sacrifice of ourselves! Without this personal sacrifice, we will never be able to pour out on souls the graces of the Sacrifice of Jesus. Our life is very short and we have to be so penetrated with the spirit of our priesthood, that our life is nothing less than a life of victim, all consumed for souls... Cost what it may, *paratum cor meum*, my heart is ready."

Biographical Sketch

Along with the reigning Pontiff, Pope St. Pius X, Father Poppe devoted much effort to the sanctification of children through catechetical instruction and Eucharistic devotion. He was assigned the work of teaching catechism at St. Coleta and discovered he had a wonderful gift for teaching children and training catechists in what he called, the "Eucharistic method" of catechesis. Within a year of his ordination, he founded the League of Communion of Children for the purpose of loving Jesus, sanctifying oneself, and setting a good example for others. The Eucharistic Heart of Jesus was the fount of grace for this movement and, by June of 1917, Father Poppe's parish saw piety flourish and the League increase to 90 children. Ever attuned to the integral link between the Heart of Jesus and the Eucharist, Father Poppe had the joy of giving first communion to twenty-one children on the Feast of the Sacred Heart, 1917.

After two years of fervent but overwhelming priestly ministry in the parish of St. Coleta, Father Poppe suffered the first in a series of heart attacks on May 11, 1919, which necessitated that he be given an assignment where he could receive more rest and care. As spiritual director to the Sisters of Charity in Moerzeke and chaplain at their home for the aged, sick, and orphaned, he continued to suffer serious relapses and was often bedridden. Despite his illness, Father Poppe spent much time in Eucharistic adoration and established the Belgian branch of the Eucharistic Crusade of Pope Pius X from his sickbed. When his health permitted it, Father Poppe would go to the parish church to make a holy hour, and children, seeing him there before the Blessed Sacrament, noticed how this young priest always smiled at Jesus present in the tabernacle. Attracted to this smiling young priest, the children were soon enrolled in Father

Poppe's catechism lessons, which he was able to teach once more. Edward's spirituality was imbued with joy and by smiling at Our Lord he was expressing his heartfelt acceptance and love of the will of God.

His priestly heart felt a profuse outpouring of spiritual concern for souls, out of which came a large number of articles, books, and letters concerning evangelization in the face of rising secularism, Marxism, and materialism. He was a man of deep prayer, living always in the presence of Our Lord, while also feeding his mind with books on theology, Mariology, spirituality, and the lives of the saints. Indeed, a turning point in Edward's spirituality was his visit to the tomb of St. Thérèse Martin in 1920 where, according to his own testimony, he received "the greatest grace of his life"—the Little Way of the Little Flower. This newly found source of spiritual strength gave courage to Father Poppe at a time when it seemed that all of his hopes and dreams for the apostolate had been thwarted by his chronic illness. By reexamining his heart and soul in relation to the proposals he had made for himself in seminary, he came to understand that his primary work was to sanctify himself so that every little action of his might be infused with grace.

A few years later, as his health stabilized, Father Poppe was reassigned to be spiritual director to priests and seminarians fulfilling their mandatory military service as orderlies and infirmarians in the Red Cross for the armed services. Father Poppe nurtured the spiritual life of the next generation of priests under his care and enjoined them always to "comfort Jesus. Take your crucifix and kiss the Five Wounds in reparation. Above all, embrace the Heart that has suffered so much from the sins of today." The tremendous witness and preaching of this young priest, bearing the sufferings of his daily cross, touched the hearts of many. Father Poppe also helped establish a community of cloistered Carmelite nuns near the base so that all would benefit from these consecrated women offering their lives of oblation and prayer.

It was Bl. Marie Deluil-Martiny, a fellow Belgian and foundress of the Congregation of the Daughters of the Heart of Jesus, who helped establish the Association of Victim Souls, among whom was counted Father Poppe. He saw his priesthood inseparable from his victimhood, seeking to sanctify his own life and aid in the sanctification of his parishioners and fellow priests. He wrote: "I burn for the coming of the reign of God in priestly souls. I burn, but I am so poor that I will be consumed before the coming of the desired reign." Father Poppe developed a special relationship and friendship with the Daughters of the Heart of Jesus at Berchem, whose charism was to promote devotion to the Sacred Heart and pray for priests. In one letter to the Sisters he wrote: "I implore you, then, in the name of the entire priesthood, the mystical Heart of Jesus: be generous, come to our aid."

The cult of Eucharistic devotion and the Sacred Heart have common characteristics which are preeminent in each devotional movement. In the Belgian church, the all-male League of the Sacred Heart (*Ligue du Sacré-Coeur*) was a driving force for the promotion of frequent, devotional reception of the Eucharist in reparation for the sins of mankind which wound the Sacred Heart. Father Poppe's bishop, Cardinal Mercier, was an avid supporter of this movement throughout the First World War, wherein empathy and sympathy could be found for the war-torn country in the suffering Heart of Jesus. In 1917, Father Poppe wrote the following words reflecting both his love for the Blessed Sacrament and the Sacred Heart: "That Host is my

Biographical Sketch

God, my Creator... my Master... my Bridegroom! He sees me... He thinks about me... He loves me... What else could He do? For God is love. I may not be worthy of it, but He is love!"

For this young priest, every liturgical action was a sacred moment, by which the priest allows others to see God's love present in him and thus experience it themselves. Father Poppe's own nation of Belgium holds the blessed distinction of being the first country to be consecrated to the Sacred Heart of Jesus on December 8, 1875, and, later that year, the cornerstone of the Sanctuary of the Sacred Heart was laid in Berchem-lez-Anvers. During the lifetime of Father Poppe, Belgium was again consecrated to the Sacred Heart by Cardinal Mercier, in the presence of the King and Queen, after the ravages of World War I.

Father Poppe lived and preached with a loving zeal for the souls entrusted to his paternal care. Urged to reawaken the waning faith, hope, and love of his countrymen, he prayed earnestly: "O my Jesus! Where are You still loved? My poor Jesus, where do You still find a heart to rest Your tired head? My poor Savior, I seek souls that console You, souls that delight You: alas! they leave You, while You are there waiting for them, Your hands full of mercy." He hoped that many would become "consolers of the pierced Hearts of Jesus and Mary. They are so unloved."

Father Poppe, his state of health demanding further rest and convalescence, returned to Moezeke on December 23, 1923, where he remained for the final six months of his short life. Undergoing subsequently more severe heart attacks, with brief interludes of improvement, Father Poppe suffered with great peace and confidence. His lifelong devotion to Mary and the Rosary was characterized by his understanding of her as a living monstrance for Jesus, by which she was

Biographical Sketch

the preeminent channel of God's graces (the title Mediatrix of All Graces being a special devotion of his). As Father Poppe's fatal condition grew evident, many came to visit the invalid in his room, among whom was an elderly woman who besought from him some souvenir or image by which to remember him. The young priest, handing her the crucifix by his bed, said: "Here is my picture, pray that I will be like it!" On his sickbed, Father Poppe was plagued by doubts regarding his priestly ministry—whether he had done enough to advance the Kingdom of God on earth—but his steadfast living of the Little Way of St. Thérèse meant his confidence in God's loving mercy never wavered. Just before his death, Father Poppe was asked by a priest friend whether he would like to live longer. With conviction, Father Poppe replied that he was offering himself as a victim "for you, for my spiritual sons, and for all the priests."

UNDER THE GAZE OF GOD

On the morning of June 23, 1923, Father Poppe celebrated his final Holy Mass, after which he was confined to bed. The following morning, while preparing for Mass, he suffered yet another heart attack and was again given the Last Sacraments by the parish priest. From this time on he was confined to bed, and suffered another heart attack on January 1, 1924, followed by a more serious relapse on February 3. A faithful servant of Jesus to the end, Father Poppe on June 10, 1924 was received into the eternal embrace of that Heart he loved so much, imitated so dearly, and preached so ardently. His last earthly moments united him to his Eucharistic Lord in Extreme Unction and, with a look of loving surrender at the statue of the Sacred Heart nearby, he surrendered his soul to God at the age of 33. "I never asked the Lord that I might live to an old age," he said, "but only that men might love Him and that priests might become holy."

Biographical Sketch

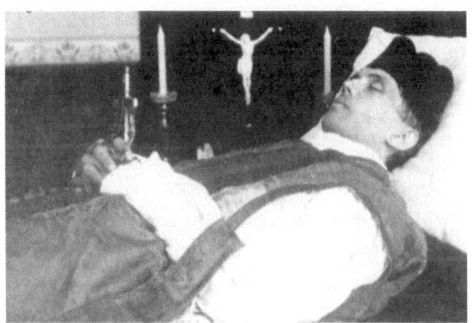

Beloved by so very many who mourned the death of this young priest and martyr for love, his bishop, Cardinal Mercier, shared their grief, revealing that there were two people during his lifetime that had shone with profound holiness: Pope Pius X and Father Poppe. In an intimate and loving letter, Cardinal Mercier wrote to Poppe's mother, saying:

> You could not have wished for a more amiable and more virtuous son. He bore Christ not only in his soul, but in his language and in his features; one could not enter into conversation with him

without feeling better. May the Sacred Heart grant you the grace to accept your trial courageously. My condolences will naturally consist in offering the Holy Sacrifice of the Mass for his intention, but I will not hesitate to call on his intercession, because I am convinced that your beloved son was a saint and that the God of Peace already has welcomed him into glory.

This warm tribute eloquently captured the essential qualities that had animated the life of Bl. Poppe: the Sacred Heart, the Holy Eucharist, the Sacrifice of the Mass, the immolation of the life of one in love with Love Itself. For six days, large crowds of devotees came to pray before the body of this holy man and recommend themselves to his prayers. His funeral Mass was attended by over two hundred priests of the diocese. He was buried in his hometown of Moerzeke on June 16, 1924. His grave became a place of pilgrimage,

Biographical Sketch

particularly for priests, who find in the holy life of Father Poppe a strength and support in their own struggles. The diocesan process for his beatification was opened on December 12, 1945, with papal approval given for his beatification in 1959. A voluminous amount of testimony was received from ecclesiastical authorities and laity — including the King and Queen of Belgium — attesting to the extraordinary holiness of Father Poppe. The most eloquent homily of Father Edward is his own life. The effectiveness of Father Poppe's apostolate was rooted in a deep interior life, whereby the heart of this priest personally knew the merciful love of God and translated it into an effective love for his fellow man. The strength of his apostolate came from his contemplative love for the Eucharist, especially the celebration of the Holy Mass, where he participated intimately in the self-giving action of our Savior's Sacred Heart.

UNDER THE GAZE OF GOD

Father Poppe's life was not easy but, in the midst of his sufferings, he understood how to conform his priesthood more closely to Christ's. It is that one holy priesthood that is shared by all the priests of the Church throughout the ages. Today, when we see the crisis of faith and identity in the lives of so many priests, religious, and laity, Blessed Poppe can be a source of inspiration and grace. Let us pray that, through the intercession of Blessed Edward Poppe, we may learn from Christ how to offer ourselves to Him completely and have a more tender devotion to our Blessed Lady, in the midst of all our joys and sorrows. We give thanks to Almighty God for the life and gift of Blessed Edward Poppe—priest, saint, and lover of the Sacred Heart.

Counsels
for
Perfection

Carry your cross

"The one who wants to be My disciple must renounce himself, take up his cross and follow Me...."

O my divine Master, you addressed this word to everyone without exception. How few have the courage to meditate on it in all honesty! How few remember it at the moment when the trial comes to disrupt their lives!

Oh Jesus, at least we will have the heart to understand it, and live it.

Spiritual reading

To read out of simple curiosity exposes you to the risk of taking on too many ideas at once. The words don't have time to sink in. Never have I read with more satisfaction and fruit than reading in God's holy presence, in small doses, with calm and recollection.

Veni Sancte Spiritus! Come Holy Spirit, enlighten my mind, prepare my heart to understand and to follow your inspirations and your desires.

Blessed Virgin Mary, come to my aid.

Prayer and mortification

Lord, how can it be that we who pray much, who receive Communion so frequently, remain so irascible, so distracted in prayer, so full of imperfections, almost as much as at the beginning of our spiritual lives?

How does it happen that the conversion so long desired is not accomplished and that the good achieved amounts to so little?

Isn't it because we mortify ourselves too little, bear too little humiliation and suffering? Prayer and frequent Communion don't give us holiness, but only grace, which is power and light to tend toward sanctity by the heroic effort of each day. Grace is for the soul what the wood and coal are for the hearth.

Through mortification and courageous effort, we must make use of grace to practice virtue, for fear of suffering from the cold in a house abundantly provided with firewood. Prayer and grace in no way diminish the effort to be made; they give us strength and enthusiasm to overcome difficulty. A cross loses the majority of its weight when it is fully accepted.

O Lord, we often ask that we may suffer and die for love of you ... and we find the littlest crosses you send us too heavy. Help me, Lord! I promise you that I will bravely go through all trials without letting the least sign of discouragement appear on my face.

Peace

My God, a victory won at the cost of a difficult and painful effort, a humiliation accepted without complaint, a mortification borne with love gives more peace to my poor soul than the best meal, the most flattering praise, or the satisfaction of all my whims. Oh Jesus, give me often the occasion to bear with patience an undeserved reproach, to repress a feeling of anger. Very often it costs me to keep silent, to not justify myself when I am right.

How can I not endure with love all the injustices done to me... the way You did. Since we have only *one* life.

Gaudete in Domino
Rejoice in the Lord

Good Master, exuberance is not true joy. You love a joyful spirit, but you also seek recollected souls. Jesus, it seems to me that my soul is never more joyous than on the days when my heart maintains its recollection in your presence. Then the bursts of laughter, the noisy animation disappears and I find myself satisfied with people and content with my fate. Our inner joy then radiates subtly on our countenance, showing in our words and communicating itself to all around us.

My God, grant me the grace to lead this recollected life in union with You. Then my soul, filled with your joy, will easily find the words of comfort to speak at the sickbed of those who are ill and miserable.

Serenity or haste?

St. Francis de Sales said, "Haste is the ruin of devotion." Peace, calm, serenity, these are the true atmosphere of piety.

Haste does not leave us the time to be recollected before prayer. Haste agitates, disturbs, and muddles us during prayer. Haste leaves us preoccupied, discontent, and drained after prayer.

Peace, calm, and serenity place the soul in God's presence before prayer. These dispositions give the soul rest in God through a full surrender to Him during prayer. They allow the soul to be united to God in the midst of all the labors, conversations, and events after prayer.

Haste wants to be heard right away. Peace wants only God and waits for God's timing in everything.

There are some who are not careful enough about their salvation and that is miserable. There are some who are too careful about their salvation and that is harmful. The latter have too little trust in God and too much anxiety about themselves. It's helpful for them to close their eyes about the future, and meditate on God's love — dying because He loves them — and not reason or be anxious about what state their souls are in, whether fervent or tepid. My inerrant Bible says of You, "God is love." The saints, who see more clearly than we do, repeat to us, "God wants our salvation more than we do." I trust in You! Make me aware, deeply aware of Your love.

To love the Cross

To suffer well, we must appreciate suffering. To appreciate suffering, we must often look at Jesus on the cross, in silence and with love. Then we recognize that we are unable to suffer by ourselves, and ask, with complete peace and serenity, for the grace to love suffering. Moreover, we should welcome all inconveniences, all the sufferings of body and heart. We should embrace simply, but with decision, all the little crosses of our state in life throughout the day, resting in the certainty that in the future the grace will be there to help us to bear the big crosses.

Charity is not weakness

My God, many times, under the pretext of love of neighbor, we sacrifice your glory and our spiritual perfection!

So often we call the fear of displeasing others "charity." Nonetheless, the true manner of loving someone frequently consists in telling him a hard truth, in revealing to him, without beating around the bush, a fault we observe in him.

To agree, so as to not displease, with the words of someone who is revealing his neighbor's faults is to give him our approval. It's not a sign of charity, but of weakness.

To follow the faulty habits and customs of one's milieu, in order to not be viewed badly, is cowardice.

A good example given with humility, whatever it may cost, is the greatest service we can render and therefore, the real love.

Oh Jesus, give me this genuine, this courageous love.

O Crux, ave
Hail, holy Cross

Lord, every Christian is your disciple. Following your example, supported by grace, he must suffer. Lord, every Religious and every priest should be a friend of the cross.

With the light of your grace, I remember always that life on earth is not meant for seeking satisfactions and pleasures.

As a Christian, on the way to an eternal happiness, I will not find my happiness in this valley of tears.

All the same, my dear Master, sometimes I discover my thoughts straying in search of personal satisfaction, seeking a little word of praise, a gesture of esteem, evidence of affection from those around me, or a feeling of sweetness and consolation in prayer.

Lord, give me consolation and peace if it is salutary for me. But above all, give me a love of and a taste for penance and the cross.

Communia non communiter
Common things, uncommonly well

St. John Berchmans had as his motto, "Do nothing extraordinary, but do ordinary things with extraordinary perfection."

Lord, grant me the grace to put this wise maxim into practice.

One does not gain more merit by being a professor in a renowned school than in fulfilling the functions of a vicar in a little village.

Running errands, cleaning, washing, ironing, are, in general, as meritorious as giving conferences or teaching.

What gives all the value to our actions is the love, courage, and fidelity with which we do them.

There is often more merit in repressing a word on our lips than in taking the discipline; bearing an undeserved reproach and not justifying oneself is certainly more painful than wearing a hair shirt; treating a proud man, an unbearable character, with patience is more meritorious than sleeping on the floor.

Fidelity in little things

The person who fulfills his duties of state with promptness and perseverance, without human respect as well as without ostentation, gives evidence of a greater perfection than the person who spends a night in prayer before the Blessed Sacrament.

O Lord, we are often seeking holiness where it is not to be found. We expect exceptional opportunities from You, and we let the thousand little daily opportunities go by. The great penances attract us, and we scorn the hundred little mortifications that demand fidelity to our rules. Nevertheless, fidelity in little things is a characteristic note in the life of all the saints.

Lord, give me today many occasions to please You and the grace to see them. Without your grace I can do nothing; with your grace I can do all things!

Weak, but trusting

The person who only sees his weaknesses and faults easily loses courage. The person who, fully aware of his weaknesses, recalls at the same time your omnipotence and your infinite mercy, that person will have the courage and strength to do everything.

Many know this truth and meanwhile think and live as if your grace counted for little, as if they were through themselves and on their own the artisans of the important work to be accomplished.

O Jesus, lift the veil that covers my eyes and the shackles that bind my heart! May I say with St. Paul, "Lord, without your grace I am nothing." I rejoice to know my weakness so well: in fact this knowledge keeps me humble, and humility ensures the presence of your divine omnipotence in my soul.

Counsels for Perfection

Noli timere
Why be afraid?

My trust is the measure of my love.

"There is no fear in love," says St. John: *timor non est in caritate*.

My God, how could I fear You for so long, fearing death and your judgment, when I consider that, having no need of me, You have called me into existence nevertheless!

My God, I cannot fear You when I contemplate and behold You nailed to the cross, when I see You suffering and dying to win my ungrateful soul.

My God, I forget all my fear and distrust. I melt with joy and love when I look at the tabernacle and in my soul I repeat these words, "That Host is my God, my creator... my Master... my Bridegroom! He looks at me... He thinks of me... He loves me...."

How could He act otherwise? "God is love." I don't deserve it... but He is love!...

Confide, fili mi
Have confidence, my child

Thérèse of the Child Jesus, teach us to throw ourselves into the arms of the compassionate Jesus after our sins and discouraging relapses with the confidence of toddlers.

The reason we are discouraged or grieve after a fall or a relapse is that we still don't sufficiently comprehend what tenderness, what compassion, and comfort God's mercy contains. This is what makes us constantly go back over previous sins, confessions, and acts of repentance.

Ah! Jesus, teach my heart to experience your ineffable mercy, so that I may humbly go there to find rest in my defeats and in my relapses.

Willing is power!

There are many who like humility, but among these there are very few who like humiliations!

Many desire suffering, but rare are those who know how to embrace the little crosses which teach them to suffer.

Many love and desire the spirit of prayer.... But who loves spiritual dryness, arid prayers, painful interior abandonment? Nevertheless these are the means which open the way of true, interior, and divine prayer... to union with God.

Many Religious aspire to the sanctity of their state, but rare are those who passionately love their Rule, the path indicated by God to guide them to it.

Many want to reach perfection, but for attaining it they count too much on themselves, too little on God.

"Today is the day of salvation"

To delay is to omit. A good word should not be deferred until tomorrow, but spoken today; not this afternoon, but this morning; not soon, but right now. "I will begin to lead a holy life at the next retreat." No. "*Ecce nunc coepi....*" I am beginning now.... The first task I will accomplish with joy, for love of You, Jesus! This very day I will raise my heart to You a hundred times, with all the fervor of which I am capable!... Today I will treat annoying people with courtesy. This very day, because to put it off is to risk not doing it at all!

"Lord, teach us to pray"

"Father, in the past I could pray with so much fervor; I delighted in my prayers! But now this is not happening: I can't say a *Pater* without distractions. The morning and evening prayers, the prayers for Communion and the others, all suffer the same fate: distraction, aridity, coldness!"

"My child, the spirit of prayer is a grace. Do you sometimes ask for this from God?"

"Oh! Yes, but without success!"

"Not without success, but you don't yet know how to use it."

"How to acquire it, then?"

"Make a particular point of it in your examination of conscience. In the morning, on rising, say resolutely, 'My God I will say all my prayers today with great care. Before each prayer—even if it is only an arrow prayer—I will wait a moment, I will put myself in your presence and I will say slowly, 'Oh my God, you are here, close to me; you hear each one of the words I will pronounce.' Then I will begin my prayer slowly. 'Our...Father...who....'

"Make a knot in your handkerchief, so you don't forget *during the day*; tangle up your rosary, fold your napkin toward you, etc., so that you think of it. In the evening, you will ask yourself: Have I thought of it? Have I waited before starting? Did I pray slowly?

"If you pray like this, you will not be able to say even half of your prayers, and you will be obliged to omit certain habitual prayers. That is nothing; half an Our

Father prepared and prayed thus is better and more beneficial than a whole rosary prayed without attention. Prayer is a dialogue with God and not the repetition of a parrot."

"I am doing this with all the generosity you advised. However, it is not working. Always this dryness!"

"Occasionally change prayers and prayer books. For example, take *The Imitation of Christ*. Place yourself in the presence of God and tell yourself again that it is God himself who is giving you the advice you are reading in this book. For example, 'My daughter, carry the cross and the cross will carry you.' Hear this divine word with a recollected heart. Let it be repeated several times by God's gentle voice. 'My daughter... carry the cross...' and so on.

"Stop at that word, as long as it seems beneficial for you. Then you will move on to another. 'My child, be courageous and full of trust... at the right time.' You will hear Jesus who is addressing these words to you personally and you will let them sink into your heart full of desire, like a balm. Continue to hear them with joy, repeat those consoling words — and answer as gently as Jesus, 'Oh, Jesus, oh my Bridegroom... how You love me!... I didn't know it!... I forgot it.... Oh Master, I thank you. I will be courageous.' The whole day one of these words will remain on your lips, and you will sigh, 'Oh Master, I thank you. I will be courageous.' Do the same with the words of the Gospel. But really look at Jesus and listen with recollection."

"This also helped for a while in the past, but now, it is long forgotten as well. Despite all my efforts, I remain always dry and without fervor!"

"My child, tell me, can you undertake a big penance? Can you bear an undeserved reprimand joyfully? Can you sometimes hold back a word that was going to fall from your lips? Can you put only one grain of salt on a bland dish? Can you be silent about the faults of others? Can you practice mortification? If not, that is probably the cause of your aridity, since prayer requires mortification; without mortification it remains insipid and dry."

"Just as in good years in the past, I have not ceased to do penances and nevertheless I remain hard as a stone."

"My child, rejoice. Your aridity is a test. You are an elect soul. Your prayer should consist in submission to your condition, as it is, and in repeating slowly, with serenity and resignation, 'Oh, my Jesus, may your will be done!... This aridity is welcome to me, even if it lasts my whole life.' Have confidence, soon you will ascend to a more perfect prayer and to an intimate union. Trust!"

Counsels for Perfection

Ambula coram me et esto perfectus
Walk in my presence and be perfect

An excellent means to advance in the path of perfection is the practice of the presence of God. In the morning, upon waking, place yourself in silence under the gaze of God. Kneel for a moment before Him. "My Lord... My God... I adore You... I acknowledge my nothingness before You...."

Remain under the benevolent gaze of God, pray under the gaze of God, frequently stop all work and close your eyes to feel the sweet divine gaze resting on you.... "Oh, my God, I consecrate to You my soul... my body...."

At the first sound of the bell, as to God's call, hasten to accomplish the prescribed exercises. At table, eat under the gaze of God. "My God... the salt is missing... I accept this privation for you." "This dish is tasteless... I will eat more of it—for you, my God." I will take less of that dessert, "for you, My God." I will greet this person in a friendly way: "Can I show indifference when you are gazing at me, my God?" Someone gives me an undeserved reproach: "My God, this cross is so easy to bear when you are near me." "Can I complain when discomforts, illness, trials affect me and I feel your gaze on me? When I am near you like a child close to his Father?"

The practice of the presence of God makes our faults imperceptibly vanish, the way the sun melts the snow; it makes virtues blossom the way spring sun makes the flowers bloom.

Ego sum panis vivus
I am the living bread

Oh Jesus, I am coming from Communion.... You are in me...You!

My priestly word made you present, at the consecration of the Mass...in these same hands which now, full of gratitude, write these words.... My hands carried You to my mouth, which love rendered mute.... And now...oh! Now...it is You.... You, my God, are in my soul!

Panis vivus vitam praestans homini! Living bread...You who give me life, You are the food of my poor soul and you make it live with Your own life.... Jesus, You feed it with Your own thoughts. You incline its desires to conform them to Yours. You nourish it in such a way that its entire life belongs to You, is inspired and directed according to Yours. *Praesta meae menti de te vivere.* Jesus, may my soul live with Your life. *In te spem habere, te diligere.* May it live with trust in You and love for You.

Grant that during this day no other food enters my soul, any earthly thought, desire, or wish. Remain in me, oh Bread of Life! Let Your example and Your lessons be to me food full of Your power. You stay in me by Your grace; I stay close to you too, like a child in the arms of his mother. I am weak too, like a child who is far from its mother. Close to You, I am as tranquil as a child who sees its mother. Oh! Abide in me and may I abide in You!

The kingdom of God is taken by force!

We must acquire a Christian mindset for battle, a brave and virile spirit. For this, we must look life's burdens and difficulties in the face, and not childishly turn our backs on them and beg to be spared. To do this, we must also tackle the challenges, wherever they come from, whether of the body or the soul, and fight as a valiant Christian against temptations and conquer them bravely, *"fortiter et suaviter,"* with courageous boldness and sweet confidence in the divine mercy.

For heaven belongs to the courageous who never say, "I will try," but always "I will."

Esto mitis!
Be meek!

Be meek, be gentle!

Lord, help me to be meek with those who seem obstinate or unbearable. Experience has taught me that it is only through meekness and self-control that we obtain results we did not hope for, while anger and even a justified answer most often fail to achieve their goal....

Jesus, meek and humble of heart, make my heart like unto Thine!

Lord, teach me to be silent in the face of the reproaches I am given. Teach me to hear with a recollected contentment hard, undeserved words. Give me a new heart, for so often mine suddenly gets angry before I succeed in calming it.

Ave Maria

Love of the Blessed Virgin produces a marvelous tenderness in our whole spiritual life. Little by little, this love enriches our heart with a sentiment of trust and submission previously unknown. It leads us step by step to the joyful acceptance and love of the many trials which beset us.

O Mary, I owe you so much! May I always be grateful to you. O Mary, I love you, I love you . . . forgive my negligence.

The one who loves Mary follows the path of salvation; the one who disdains her love, even if he had the gift of miracles, does not deserve any trust. Why yield to fear still when we love Mary with a sincere love? The person whom Mary has won to her love remains always held in the net of her affection, and the more the devil tries to tear him away from her influence, the more the net of the Virgin closes around him to protect him. Mother like no other, Mother most admirable, pray for us!

"*O quam suavis es!*" Why is it that the servants of Mary obey in everything with such joyful simplicity? What is it that gives them such filial tenderness in their relations with God? Why are they so understanding, so kind and friendly with the worst people in the same way? O Mary, it is you; through the maternal protection with which you enfold them, you communicate to them, without their knowledge, your signature humility and your unequalled sweetness.

Be a martyr!

Lord, I do not ask for any other martyrdom than to accomplish each day in perfection all the duties of my state in life. I ask for no other mortification than that occasioned all the time by dealings with difficult, ungrateful, and unreasonable people, who give me at every moment the opportunity to practice it.

Many wish to die as martyrs, but they reject the martyrdom of each day's problems and of daily duties. A frequent illusion: we aspire to a life of exceptional sacrifice and refuse the smallest mortifying obligations, such as silence about the faults of others, observing the discipline of the convent, forgiving hurtful words and offensive treatment.

Illusion. Yes, my God, illusion.

A punishment is a reward, a cross is a crown.

Break the bonds!

What are you still attached to? To this person, to that concern, to this pleasure, to that consolation? One must be ready to break all bonds, for fear of never being completely attached to Jesus.

It is folly to think over the past too much, as well as to be worried too much about the future. "Each day's trouble is sufficient...," the Lord cautions us. Let us be content to accomplish today our little duties of state perfectly.

Guard your tongue!

The fault which even perfect souls conquer last is speaking of the faults of others (Scaramelli, *Spiritual Direction*).

In order to live in a truly recollected manner we must live in God's presence and speak with Him a great deal.

"The one who does not sin in speech is perfect," says St. James.

The one who can't be silent will never be perfectly recollected; the one who is not recollected will never be perfect. The perfect man is never verbose. He finds his comfort much more in keeping silent than in speaking for no reason.

Become a saint

"A religious who does not intend to become holy is a fool," said Fr. Valentine Paquay.[*]

---

[*] Fr. Valentin Paquay, OFM, servant of God. Died in Hasselt, Belgium in 1905.

Certainly many think, "I want to become a saint...," but few say, "I will become a saint." Nevertheless it is this definite word, "I will," that Jesus expects from us, to take us by the hand and help us to climb the steep path. Many do not dare to utter the definitive word because at bottom they are counting on themselves, and because, blinded by fear of suffering and conscious of their weakness, they lose sight of the power of grace and the sweet and mysterious comfort Jesus gives.

Oh Jesus, help us to make the decision to become saints in all sincerity.

Nihil sum et nescivi!
I am nothing and I do not know!

Oh my God, if your grace did not keep me in the right path at every moment, I think that left to myself I would fall into the worst faults.

May you be blessed for that precious protection with which you surround me in occasions of sin.... May you be blessed, You who do not leave me for an instant when danger threatens! Blessed also for making me feel so profoundly the great weakness and inclination to sin which really belong to me. This knowledge is a great motivation for humility in your presence and allows me from that moment to count on your omnipotent grace and your inexhaustible mercy even more.

Oh Lord, humility becomes easy when you make us experience your presence. Then we understand that our whole life is conditioned by your omnipotent ubiquity. We feel with a sweet certainty that it is only through you that we have life, movement, and being and that before you we are only nothing! This feeling of our littleness produces in us a great and sweet humility, a holy confidence in your paternal aid, a deep contempt for ourselves, and in consequence, a calm but firm desire for humiliation.

What can be less than nothing? Oh infinite and good God, help me to live always in your almighty presence.

When I think that I who depend entirely on You, who am nothing without You ... I use the life and powers you gave me, to offend you ... so often!

Oh God, who are so good, I see now the evil of my sins.... How can I still refuse to agree to your requests, even just once? Are you not the master of my self ... the absolute master? .... Oh, please help me to live always by this truth.

Wasn't it you who said, "Without me you can do nothing for your salvation"? And St. Paul, "I can do all things in the One who strengthens me."

Oh Jesus, what cause for humility! And what a source of infinite trust and endless courage!

I no longer want to rely on myself, oh my Jesus. Instead, I will willingly hear humiliating words and reproaches addressed to me.

In cruce salus!
Salvation comes from the Cross

Lord, this week I intend to carry my cross with particular recollection. Each time I trace the sign of the cross over my heart, I will think, "Lord, I accept the cross, whatever it may be.... Isn't the cross the Christian symbol, my symbol? The trial which surprises me: this humiliation, this loneliness, this spiritual dryness, this mortification, this uncertainty which worries me... all this is my cross. I accept it without reserve, with all my strength. I accept it with joy since your grace is all-powerful."

Yes, my God, I am going in the wrong direction when I seek perfection in other ways than the way of the cross. And I am mistaken when I look for means more fitting than those which come to me from the cross for the conversion of souls, for consoling the afflicted.

Therefore, let my motto be: "*In cruce salus.*" My salvation is in the Cross!

Come and follow Me!

Oh Jesus, here are the words by which you invited me to leave the world to follow you.

"Come and follow Me." It is good to follow *You*, as you ask me and not to follow this person or that person. You didn't say, "Follow some doubtful customs of perfection, and live in conformity with prevailing ideas." No, You said, "Follow *Me!* I am the Way, follow Me; I am the Truth, listen to My voice; I am the Life, live your life in imitation of Mine.

Read my Gospel; there you will find the true Christian spirit. Read the lives of the saints, there you will find the true application of my teaching.

Guided by an enlightened confessor, imitate them and follow the inspirations I give you in these readings.

Veni, sponsa mea!... My beloved bride, come!"

Tristis es anima mea...
My soul is filled with sorrow...

O divine martyr of Gethsemane, Your soul also was acquainted with sadness and interior suffering! In the Garden of Olives, you experienced this strange feeling of abandonment; no one consoled you and a mortal weariness overcame you....

"*Coepit tardare et maestus esse,*" Jesus was seized with weariness and sadness. How these words strengthen me, now that the same feeling — so painful — of inner solitude afflicts me, and an inescapable sadness envelops me like a veil of mourning and fills my heart with repugnance.

O sweet consolation. You too, oh my Jesus, you suffered in an identical manner.

UNDER THE GAZE OF GOD

I rejoice to endure with you this suffering, ignored, unknown, and misunderstood by all. This bitterness becomes sweet to me now; this solitude brings me close to you. O my divine Master, do not spare me; give me suffering, still more suffering... and help me to love that suffering! Because I know, oh my Jesus, that you lift all the weight from the heaviest burden at the moment the trial is fully accepted. For the heart which loves the cross, you have a mysterious balm, and for the mouth that utters the *fiat*, an unimagined sweetness.

How strong is the one who loves the cross!... No, my Jesus, I only ask you for strength to bear it well... always more strength and a deeper humility, in order to be in a state to bear a heavier cross. My cross becomes unnoticeable from the moment that your grace makes me love it. In your chalice of suffering, sadness is on the surface but at the bottom is peace.

Trial or chastisement?

Lord, never again will I ask myself the question if my sadness of soul, my illness, my misfortune constitutes a trial or a punishment.

Many say, and I am among them—alas!—"Oh, If only I was sure that it is a trial and not a punishment. I would accept with enthusiasm this anxiety, that misfortune, and I would wish to have them all my life." O Lord, they are ignoring that it is precisely in this that the painful side of the trial resides, and also the merit: not to know if it is truly a cross.

No, my Jesus, it's enough for me to know that it makes me suffer to infer its salvific power and keep intact all my tranquility of soul. All other considerations are "out of season"; they are only good for making us melancholics.

If this misfortune which comes to me is a punishment, I accept it out of love and right away I will be reconciled with

You; if it is a trial, it brings me near to You, and creates for me the ideal path to a life of humility and recollection.

Passions or the cross?

Passions are sweet in the mouth, but bitter in the heart. The cross is sweet in the heart, but terribly bitter in the mouth.

For the cross, the appetite comes in eating it: we begin with nausea, we continue with desire. Passion begins with desire, but ends with disgust.

No one can believe the sweetness of the cross, except the person who isn't afraid to experience it in depth.

Mary, queen of martyrs, help me!

"But Jesus was silent…"

Lord, I want to sign a contract between my heart and my tongue. Each time my heart is under the sway of anger, I will remain silent. Yes, completely silent. If it happens that, despite my efforts, my heart is agitated and carried away, I will keep silent my tongue at least, in the hope that subduing it quickly, my heart will also be silent.

"The one who does not sin in speech is perfect."

O Lord, a hero's courage is required for this sometimes. Please grant it to me, You who kept silence before the tribunal of Caiaphas and Herod.

Everything becomes possible to the one who cooperates with your grace.

For the hours of aridity

Oh painful and difficult moments! Jesus has come into me in holy Communion, and in my heart, which tepidity has reduced to powerlessness, I do not find either thought, or feeling, or speech for the One I love above all!

I remain mute, confounded, disappointed, conscious of my poverty, and the destitution of my parched soul.

Kneeling before the altar, I feel completely ashamed: I experience only coldness, dryness, and indifference!

Happily, one great resource remains to me, a means especially powerful: submission to the humiliation God is sending me. I turn my eyes to Jesus, and with all the conviction and all the sincerity of which I am capable, I say to Him, "Oh my beloved Master, I am not worthy to receive You into my utterly tepid soul... not worthy to feel consoled by the sweetness of your holy presence.... No, I am not worthy.... The barrenness which afflicts my soul, this insensibility, this sleepiness which overcomes me, I accept them as the cross which accompanies your presence in me....

"Let me embrace this cross.... Then, strengthened by love, my will can endure this interior aridity without anxiety, for as long as you please.

"I know that you permit me sorrow, not so that you may rejoice at my suffering, but only out of a motive of love — to spare me the much greater sorrow of purgatory and hell.

"Oh Jesus, now I am happy; I feel peace descend, now that I have uttered my *fiat*.

"Oh holy Virgin, I became your slave; I entrusted to you all my concerns. It is for you now to give thanks, to adore, and to love Jesus in me; I unite myself to all your affections, your prayers, and your proofs of love for Him."

And, in union with the Virgin Mary, I will recite slowly the act of charity, or a part of my morning prayer again or any other prayer... and from now on I will allow Jesus all the time to act in he pleases in me.

Obedience and humility

Obedience pleases God more than penance. Mortifying one's will is worth ten times more than mortifying one's body. And the use of chains and hairshirts is, for rebellious and proud souls, more harmful than useful. All corporal mortification which hinders the perfect accomplishment of the duties of one's state in life is prohibited and inadvisable.

The greatest mortification consists in recognizing joyfully God's will in each day's difficulties; in accomplishing the daily duties without complaint, whatever tedium accompanies them. The most meritorious mortification is punctual fidelity to the Rule and to the commands of Superiors.

Often what is far removed from the ordinary attracts us more; but the practice of perfection in the fulfillment of each day's task, in the fidelity to ordinary exercises of piety, constitutes for all the true, and for most, the only way which leads to a perfect life.

Humility, obedience, and charity render mortification pleasing to God and to us.

They are like the sauce that adds flavor to the dish.

Mortification, for the soul who boasts about it, is like a bucket which leaks: all the merits and good effects are lost.

The one who covers the faults of others with his silence has already gone a great way on the path of perfection.

The one who admits his weakness without surprise is on the path which leads to true humility.

The one who never hides the truth out of fear of displeasing others proves he is already very detached from people.

The one who helps others at his own expense proves he follows the gospel path of love for neighbor.

The one who finds his only consolation in God does not court danger for his soul.

The one who is quiet about his good qualities, just as he is about his faults, demonstrates a great spirit of mortification.

The one who joins a recollected mind with the joy of optimism shows that he practices the interior life.

The one who never speaks ill of evil doers, but shows compassion for sinners and not contempt, lives according to the mind of the Lord.

The one who is not surprised or scandalized by the imperfection of his companions will love them easily, and better.

Ama nesciri!
Gladly be unknown!

Oh Jesus, meek and humble of heart, preserve me from pride: that would be the worst calamity which could befall me. I prefer to be forgotten by all, unknown, despised, humbled to the dust rather than see myself full of smugness, raised above others. I prefer to remain little, weak, powerless rather than become a proud leader.

Oh Jesus, make my ears not so willingly hear the compliments addressed to me; let my heart remain closed to self-satisfaction in my personal affairs; let my thoughts not return constantly to victories gained, good works accomplished, praises received. May unjust judgments which I have endured, bitter criticisms of my work, humiliating treatment I have been subject to, be a consolation to me. *Ama nesciri*... love to be unknown.

When will the moment come when I will be happy to be forgotten by all, to see that no one thinks about me, except to despise me like common rubbish?

That moment will come when your grace makes me see that this is indeed the reality of things: I am nothing and I deserve nothing.

St. Joseph

St. Joseph's rank as foster father of the child Jesus and as spouse of the Mother of the Savior gives him precedence over other saints. But we are also the brothers of Jesus: St. Joseph is our foster father, just as the Virgin Mary is our spiritual Mother. St. Teresa of Avila had the custom each year of asking for a special favor on the feast of St. Joseph: she says her prayer was always heard.

Oh St. Joseph, teach me how to please Jesus and his dear Mother. For so many years you lived intimately with them! Foster Father of our souls, teach us to follow your example.

Trust and resignation

St. Thérèse said, "Have only one fear—the fear of fearing something."

Against human respect: do everything as if there was nothing in the world but God and your soul, she said.

"I want to become a great saint in a short time!" (St. John Berchmans.)

The good God wants all or nothing from a truly interior soul. Mediocrity is unbearable to Him.

If I were to die today and I was asked what I regret, I would say that I only regret one thing, and I can find nothing else: that I did not give myself more.

Ah! My God, and if I was asked then if I do not fear the judgment and how will I be calm in the face of death, it seems to me that I would find the only means for that, the truly efficacious means: I would quickly forget all the evil I had done, I would remove my thought from all the good I neglected to do, and I would stay totally in the consoling idea of your love.

My Jesus, I am happy to offer You my toothaches and illness. They make me stupid and unable to pray well, to read, and to preach to my children. Amen, Jesus! I happily suffer this "nothing" with you, for my little souls who are on retreat for their first Communion. I am sure my sufferings are more useful to them than my words.

Christo confixus sum cruci — Fixed to the cross with Christ

"Many souls have the courage to climb the hill of Calvary, but they descend before the crucifixion. We should not come down from Calvary before being crucified, and we and the cross have become inseparable. Alas! The world is filled with deserters of Calvary. Grace does not crucify a man despite himself.... Suffering has a long, slow opening and crucifixion is matter for endurance." (Father Faber)

My God, I give myself to you, I who have not even climbed Calvary, I who scarcely dare to look at the cross, and who have not yet embraced it. I will consider the austere thought that we must suffer and be fixed to the cross with you. I will recall each morning, on waking, the duty of suffering, and I will hasten to kiss your wounds on my crucifix. Each morning I will say to You, "Jesus, your cross, and the grace to love it!"

Counsels for Perfection

Mary, my Mother, I gave you everything; arrange, prepare everything in me so that I am ready for suffering. "To love without suffering is as vain as suffering without love." That is so clear! It's obvious.

As great as the peace is in this moment, so great the cross will be later! Peace prepares us, disposes us for the cross. In a period of consolation it is dangerous to forget the next cross which is coming.

My Jesus, it seems to me that a single thought should be dominant in our soul and in our entire life: the thought of Jesus, and of "Jesus Crucified," as your Apostle Paul says. Alas! Despite ourselves, we feel overpowered by another thought: the desire for rest, for consolation, for satisfaction. We aren't yet accustomed to the rigor of the gospel teaching: "Whoever wants to be My disciple must take up his cross." On the contrary, we seek to escape the cross as much as possible, to avoid illness, annoyance, humiliation, and suffering, as if you had said, "Whoever wants to be My disciple must seek joy and rest."

I beg you, Jesus, to make your bloody crucifixion so present to my soul that I am ablaze with love and with a holy ardor to follow you, so that I seek only the cross and being forgotten here below. On high, those crosses will change into glory, into happiness and bliss.

Do you fear the cross?

To keep your soul's desire directed toward heaven, you must necessarily direct it toward Calvary. "In the evening of life we will be judged on love." (St. Thérèse, quoting St. John of the Cross.) But you will love in the measure that you consent to suffer.

Felix culpa — Happy fault

Nothing honors God like confidence and I think that confidence is more pleasing to Him after a fall, after a discouraging infidelity, since then it is perfumed with humility and courage.

Divine Providence

A man's soul is more precious than his body: it is for souls above all that Christ was crucified.... Given this, what will be the primary goal of the divine solicitude in regard to us? Will it be the health, the satisfaction of the body, or rather the health and salvation of our soul? Without any doubt, it will be for the progress of our soul in the way of perfection.

Therefore, what should we ask for and hope to obtain mainly from divine Providence? Spiritual favors for our soul or temporal favors for the body?

The answer is clear: spiritual favors which benefit our soul; we can desire these and ask for them without any restriction. As for temporal favors, on the contrary, our desire and the prayer that expresses it should be conditioned by their usefulness for spiritual ends. This explains why many prayers and novenas made to obtain a healing or to win a lawsuit remain ungranted by God.

If divine Providence allows the illness to continue or the case to be lost, it is because this illness is useful, more than every other means, in our sanctification. Because of it, we exercise patience, we are destined to seclusion, and with the aid of grace, it is a school of resignation for us and of humble submission to God's will. For always, whatever happens, divine Providence helps us, as much for the soul as for the body, with wisdom and paternal solicitude. It helps us in everything that happens to us, whether spiritual or temporal, making us advance in the path of perfection and eternal salvation.

But, it will be said, aren't we permitted to pray for our healing, if we are sick? To ask for success in our business dealings ... to pray that we will be spared famine and other calamities?

Of course. But many ask for health for its own sake and prosperity out of love for riches. They ask to remain sheltered from trials so that their life may be more comfortable and agreeable.... In a word, the reason a many people desire temporal favors is fear of trials, from a phobia of the cross, and not at all the idea that, remaining protected from illness and trials, the path to heaven will be more secure for them.

Unconsciously, with many people prayer and religion are regarded as a means to ensure happiness *on earth*, and to be sheltered from many difficulties.... And meanwhile, Christ's word is, "The one who does not renounce himself and take up his cross cannot be my disciple."

From this it follows that what we should ask for in our prayer is only to be protected against such maladies, delivered from such disasters and disappointments as could hinder our progress on the way of perfection and salvation.

The universe, the succession of days and seasons, events follow their course in conformity with fixed laws which are assigned to the sun, which rules everything in nature, and to which, in a way, man is also subject. Among these events and incidents, there are a good number which afflict the human heart (such as accidents, deaths, betrayal, war). In these circumstances, what will divine Providence do for me?

For myself, I pray with passion and perseverance to obtain light and courage to bear with love and merit all these vicissitudes of my life. And God, through his divine Providence, then gives to our heart the desired sentiments of abandonment, faith, and love to endure these painful events and to make them useful for our salvation. Even more: Providence is ready

Counsels for Perfection

to resort to a special intervention to prevent this malady, that disaster, this fire, each time these trials would constitute an insurmountable obstacle to our salvation.

It is the same for the temptations of the soul, its aridity, and its afflictions. Divine Providence ordains these to make us humble, patient, trusting, and eager for perfection. God is aware of them and uses them, one by one, to benefit us day by day.

How then should we pray in the dangers and trials God sends us? Jesus teaches us by his example: "My Father, if it is possible to sanctify me without this illness, without these misfortunes, then let this chalice be taken away from me; but may your will be done in all things, and not mine...."

Conformity to God's will, and confidence in His divine Providence means that we pray and after having truly prayed, we are certain that God will either give us the graces desired to bear the trial He sends us with profit, or else can remove from us a cross which could harm our soul's well-being.

Ah! If we knew the value of our soul, if we understood the splendor of heaven, and the price of eternity... then we would understand the value of the cross and the usefulness of trials: we would be convinced that the days on which divine Providence shows the most concern for us are those when it permits suffering and trials to come to us.

In cruce salus! Our salvation is in the cross!

Sparks

I
Sanctity & Perfection

Here is holiness in a nutshell: love God's will.

Being holy is nothing more than accomplishing the Lord's holy will in everything.

The will of God is God Himself. You can adore this will just as you adore the Most Blessed Sacrament.

The will of God is loveable and makes everything sweet.

It is in God's will that one finds true peace.

To each one his job: your job is to become saints.

Become holy! This is a work which deserves the effort it costs.

With both hands, let us hold fast our resolve: to become saints.

We should not want to be "holy people," but saints.

We should become saints and in that labor we must sweat. Yes, literally, sweat at it. Holiness really deserves this.

A perfect soul does nothing by halves.

I would rather die than serve God by halves.

A religious who doesn't intend to become holy is someone who doesn't understand his vocation.

I pray for your dear convent, so that all the living stones of that spiritual edifice may be precious stones: *lapides pretiosi*, namely, humble saints. One precious stone has more value than a whole truck load of bricks.

Beware of saints who can bear nothing, of those who at a biting word or a bit of a blow, fall quickly into sadness. That is porcelain sanctity: it won't last long.

Don't place your perfection in extraordinary things or in devotions apart from the Rule: your perfection is your Rule.

Your duties of state are the authentic material of your sanctification.

Your duties of state, your crosses of state, your apostolate of state are the regular paths to sanctity, because they are the infallible realization of Jesus's will regarding you. They are, in *His* plan! And His plan is *the* plan of grace.

Do your duty and consent to God's will; this is the shortest path.

Respect for duties and for little crosses of state — in fact, this is the orthodox formula for holiness.

One holy soul is more than sufficient to revivify a whole parish.

One holy soul converts more sinners than a thousand imperfect souls.

A holy priest is the most beautiful praise you can raise to Me, Your Lord. *"Laus Deo"* — one such priest is a living benediction which rises to heaven and which descends on souls in My Church.

To obtain one priest, to sanctify a single priest, is to become the mother and source of joy for a multitude of souls.

Sanctity & Perfection

A holy priest is a sun which rises and unexpectedly illuminates, warms, and gives growth to everything. Oh my God, give us holy priests!

Jesus blesses in a special manner those who pray for his future priests.

Holy priests sanctify parishes, restore the fervor of convents, and renew vigor. They will touch hearts of stone.

A holy priest works miracles in the world of souls.

The times are so bad that saints alone can remedy them.

How can the world still be saved? Ah! It seems to me, by no other means than by holy priests.

Concerning the improvement of society, ultimately everything comes back to our sanctity.

Holiness is the best apologia for the teaching of Jesus, the best source of conviction, and the best inspiration toward a supernatural, Catholic life.

Knowledge is a precious gift, but in the end all of it is reduced to sanctity and flows into it. A saint does more, and can do more than a savant, the more prudent and modest he is.

Only the saints leave a track behind them; others make noise, but leave nothing in their wake.

The hesitant? They are at the mercy of the world.

Sanctity & Perfection

God wants all or nothing from a truly interior soul. Mediocrity is intolerable to Him.

However painful it may be, what is given remains given.

Be free! This says everything. Oh, sweet liberty which fears no one's gaze and seeks no praise! Holy liberty which makes us so joyful and so serene, and attaches us so firmly to God!

The fervent soul is the one which has a great desire for perfection, even if, perhaps, it still has many faults.

The fervent soul's desire for perfection, her will to attain it, her efforts to tend to it—this is already perfection.

The work of amendment and perfection progress step by step, rise stone by stone. Becoming holy is growing, not leaping.

UNDER THE GAZE OF GOD

You should have patience especially with yourself.... We do not be come saints in a month or a few years.

Light and consolation are rays from the other life, which help us to remain good. But it's not reasonable to want to have heaven on earth.

For those to whom Jesus one day gave the sweet and powerful attraction to perfection, there is no true joy except in the free and full accomplishment of all His desires.

In the exchange with God, we become more and more like Him. We receive into ourselves his beauty more and more, his perfection reflected and participated in our soul. We become a living praise of God, "*laus Gloriae.*"

To give glory to God is to make His perfection ours, it is to conform to Him in our thoughts, our desires, our acts; it is to radiate his life: to be beautiful and reflect his brightness.

Be saints. Through this you will yourselves be happy, and certainly you will make those around you happy.

To become holy is easy and pleasing when we have a tender and steadfast devotion to Mary.

2
The Eucharist

A day without Mass is a day without the sun.

A Mass without Communion is a celebration without food.

Find your strength in the Bread of the strong: you will not find support anywhere else.

Seek your divine Savior in the Tabernacle. Shut your eyes and open your soul, remaining humbly before Him in a surrender full of trust. Seek in union with Mary and you will find. Wait and desire with her.

Do you frequently expose yourself to the "sun"? Do you go often to sit in the "sun"? *Sol amabilis Jesus est.* The Host is this Sun of love.

In Communion the children are placed in the sun, and have themselves become little suns, through the effect of the light which penetrates them. *Luceat lux vestra!* Let your light shine.

The Victim lives His life in victim souls.

Remain *mitis et humilis*, little, meek and kind. This is what we learn before the Host, especially in dry prayer.

Our holy hour each Thursday, with our crusaders, the Sisters: an advance guard of victims! These are the ones who put everything in motion.

Divine Host, transform me wholly and completely, so that I may accomplish in souls the divine work of your heavenly Father.

3
Marian Devotion

Let us understand that devotion to Mary does not stop at her, but that it is simply, in reality, devotion to Jesus and to the Most Holy Trinity, adored in His chosen temple.

Everything comes to us through Mary: Jesus, grace, and holiness.

Do you know that in the liturgy our good Mother is called *"puteus aquarum viventium,"* the spring which causes living waters to flow? *"Fons hortorum,"* the spring which waters our garden with the fertile graces of Jesus! In the depth of your soul, draw from that spring, open it through trust and allow yourself to be inundated gently with its waters.

There, in that soul full of grace, burns the love of Jesus: there we can more surely and more fully experience its regenerating action.

Oh! May Mary keep us faithful in her love! May she gently make us die and form us anew in her divine Jesus. May we allow ourselves to be filled with light and warmth in her, and be seen henceforth as hearths of warmth for souls, for poor, dark, and cold souls, until opening to receive our rays, they themselves become light and fire.

Go with confidence to kneel before the Throne of grace: grace itself is the God-Man, His throne is Mary.

Let us seek Jesus in Mary. In her we should allow ourselves to be penetrated and entirely permeated with His priestly spirit of offering.

Marian Devotion

The little book of Louis de Montfort on *True Devotion* is a treasure. Few go to the trouble of finding it.

Pray with Mary often to learn her true and full dedication, since this is a precious grace for becoming holy and for doing good. This grace requires much humility, simplicity, and prayer. Have the attitude of Mary before Jesus.

Do not study the mystery of grace, meditate on it. Read in prayer, with a humble desire for true devotion.

Let us love Mary, our Mother, with a filial love. She is the way that leads to Jesus.

How much shorter, easier, and more secure Mary makes the path which leads to Jesus! She knows the crossings, the little paths, the secret ways.

Never be alone on the journey; that is, keep Jesus close to you, with Mary.

In devotion to Mary is found the secret of tenderness, trust, and liberty found in the piety of the saints.

The love of Mary transforms our whole life; it puts a hidden sweetness and a tenderness in our piety; it makes our work more pure and more meritorious; it leads us to Jesus in Communion; it opens for us the secrets of the Host and brings us to the Sacred Heart, to heaven.

Put a drop of Marian devotion into everything! It gives everything a sweet taste.

Overflowing good humor is a fruit of the Holy Spirit; it is especially the privilege of those who receive His gifts through the mediation of His humble Spouse.

Marian Devotion

All the same, you have a Mother! Isn't she *vita, dulcedo, et spes nostra*, our life, our sweetness, and our hope? Well, then?

Are you faithful about doing everything with Mary? Do you glance at her before each prayer, each exercise, each lesson? A precious habit: it is as if each time you opened over yourself the floodgates of grace.

Since at every instant and before every action or thought, grace is needed to render these meritorious, and since Mary is the Mediatrix of all graces, isn't it logical to have recourse to her for us to obtain them?

Love Mary as your good, your illustrious, your powerful Mother, as the one who each day causes your soul to shine brighter with new diamonds of grace, as the one who knows the secret of union with Jesus and teaches it to her children.

UNDER THE GAZE OF GOD

Do you know a good diamond cutter? I don't know one better than Mary. Entrust to her all the diamonds in your coffers. She cuts them so finely, with great precision.

Do everything with Mary and very soon you will be what you should be.

In her, allow yourself to be slain like a small lamb, by forgetting yourself, and by the painful sacrifice of yourself.

To Mary's little servants belong prayer without consolation, with distaste, distraction, weariness and dryness.

If you are united to the humble Mother of Jesus, if before each action you ask for her spirit — ah! — you can indeed keep your Jesus close to you!

Before a spiritual exercise, do you specifically place yourself under the influx of

Marian Devotion

Mary's mediation? This practice establishes in you and over you the light and love of Jesus; and it is very sweet.

Never pray alone; always invite Mary. You are then more intimately near to Jesus.

Learn to see the tabernacle with Mary's eyes, and to long for Jesus with her very humble heart.

Adore Jesus in the monstrance: Mary is the living monstrance of Jesus.

May the ardent thirst which was in Mary be in you and consume you with desire and love.

Mary is my strength, all my hope, all my trust.

With Mary the heaviest crosses are easy to bear.

UNDER THE GAZE OF GOD

With Mary all fear, all anxiety disappears from our hearts.

With Mary our hearts become humble before God, gracious for men, compassionate for the poor, and gentle for our enemies.

With Mary our piety becomes tender and filial.

Have a fervent love for Mary and you will experience sweetness in your devotion, abandonment and joy in trials, perfection and peace in your whole life.

What a desert of dryness, temptation, and doubts a person must cross who wants to go to Jesus without Mary's special support.

The person who wants to grow in holiness without Mary is like a child who wants to grow up without his mother.

Marian Devotion

Mary will cover you with her shadow, and you will remain calm and confident. She will begin the journey with you and lead you by secret shortcuts. You will not be spared suffering, but she will make you hungry for it, as if for an essential food. Ah, Mary! Mary! Her name will be like honey and balm on your lips. Mary! Mary! *Ave Maria!* Who can resist it? Tell me, who will be lost with the *Ave Maria?*

4
Faith & Trust

Frequenting the truth opens the eyes of the soul and dissipates all the mists of uncertainty.

Truth cannot restrain its brightness; it must burn and spread warmth around itself.

Be wise, but remain a child and practice what you preach.

Those who live the teaching will always be the most capable of grasping it and knowing it fully and intimately.

Live your faith. Faith triumphs over the world, as well as over our most rebellious passions.

UNDER THE GAZE OF GOD

Read the lives and writings of the saints; that is the best commentary for the study of theology, both theoretical and practical.

Nothing is sweeter or more comforting for a Christian soul than to live in the proximity of a saint.

God's undertakings work through the spirit of God and according to the power of God.

Hope without wanting to find your reasons for hope in yourself. Hope is a theological virtue, something divine, which has God for its object and motive. Hope because God is "GOD": infinitely good and all-powerful.

Trust is the measure of our love.

Love of God is indissolubly tied to trust.

Faith & Trust

Men are so often false: they deceive, they cheat. Jesus is the true friend.

Jesus always remains good, wonderfully good, even after our infidelities; but then He asks for a greater trust and a more humble generosity.

God's glory consists in pardoning and healing.

Even with grace, we do not overcome our nature in just a few months.

If the duties are painful, the graces are abundant.

A half-will, a hesitant desire, keeps the soul nearly closed: the grace of Jesus cannot penetrate except in feeble rays, as through a narrow crevice.

To fail in trust is to shut the Heart of Jesus.

Discouragement, anxiety, melancholy: all this comes from the devil. Humble, absolute trust, and serenity in interior trials or in foreseen afflictions: this comes from God. Think about this.

Distrust comes from the devil; but you must have God, not the devil, in you.

All discouragement, depression, and anxiety are the work of the devil. All joy, cheerfulness, and serenity are the fruit of filial confidence in God, through His Mother.

Remain in peace and rejoice to be purified in a dry confidence, one that is not felt: it's an excellent preparation, provided that you don't mix it with anxiety or bitterness.

If you are alone, you will never succeed. From the moment that Jesus and Mary are helping you, you are sure of your fate, on the condition that you remain trusting.

Faith & Trust

Certain people have faith as far as prayer and mortification. Few believe during trials and apparent failure. Few believe "until the end." However that faith is the weapon for our success.

Jesus doesn't resist a soul who, conscious of its weakness, takes refuge in His Heart like a child and meekly repeats to Him, "I can do all things Him who strengthens me."

God knows my weakness when I am alone. As for me, I know my strength when God is with me. I can do everything—yes, I, powerless and lukewarm—I can do everything through the power of my good Father.

God's providence is guaranteed for everything, as soon as you do what's possible for you.

UNDER THE GAZE OF GOD

What God wants, what is according to *His* plan and *His* understanding, will never lack appropriate aid.

I will have more trust in prayer and in the arrangements of Providence than in my poor calculations.

Jesus and Mary are taking care of you, and therefore no furrowed brow, no worry in your soul!

Heaven is glorious and it will last long enough to give you the courage to suffer and keep silent now.

5
Love

"*Caritas est sese dare totum Deo.*" To love is to give oneself to God, completely and without keeping anything back.

"*Et nos credidimus caritati!*" We have believed in God's love! And we delivered ourselves to that great love. For to believe is finally to give oneself, in consequence, to that faith.

Goodness seeks for open souls; He runs to them. Love never leaves love without an answer.

"*Amari et amare, en tota perfectio!*" To be loved and to love, this is the whole of perfection! Don't forget the first part, "*amari.*" Let yourself be loved by God and rejoice humbly in His love.

UNDER THE GAZE OF GOD

Let us pray that love makes us blind to everything that is not Him, and that we discover Him and value Him, and Him alone, in everything. Then we will read His name on every cross, and we will embrace the cross at the place where His name is written.

To be blind is the lover's happiness. Blessed blindness! May it be ours!

May nothing seem too costly for us to respond to love, to the infinite love of God.

Love — that is, the filial offering of ourselves — is the measure of our sanctity.

Love is the weight of each thing. And love is uprightness of will, and not feelings or consolation.

Your life has its value from love, and love is in the will and not in the feelings.

Love

Your first duty, the duty in all other duties, is a life of courageous and faithful love, with Jesus and Mary.

Let love arrange your life, your health, your future. For after all, love is love — and love cannot be anything but goodness, pure goodness.

May love be a sweet torment to you.

The love of the Heart of Jesus is your beneficent sun: it doesn't cease to illumine and purify you, even if you have ceased to be faithful. Believe in love, and let it penetrate you through the divine Sun. This is a spiritual "sun bath"; the procedure is very simple, but its effects are abundant.

Love is so tender when it is fed with true humility, and it raises its eyes toward God with such trust when it rests on the knowledge of its full and complete dependence.

UNDER THE GAZE OF GOD

Never act without an intention of love, even when you correct homework or smoke your pipe: *"quotidiana amorose!"* Accomplish with love the most ordinary things; this is a maxim of salvation.

Nothing is small in your life: everything is rendered great and precious by the "gift of yourself."

God doesn't look at the gift, but at the soul which gives it.

Jesus will ask you not so much what you did, but how you did it.

In fact, love, even not felt but simply willed, is the treasure and the soul of everything. It is the diamond which is precious, the box is valueless. The diamond is the will of God contained and hidden in the common occurrence of a headache, dryness, uncertainty, or work. Before rejecting the box

Love

in forgetfulness, let us open it and take out the diamond every time.

The person who helps another at the cost of his own advantage shows that he is walking in God's path.

There is no hatred in a Christian's heart from the moment he recalls the example of his crucified God praying for His executioners who are blaspheming Him.

There is no bitterness in the heart of a Christian who repeats frequently, "Jesus, make my heart like Yours."

The person who is not surprised or indignant about his neighbor's imperfections will be able to love him more easily and better.

The person who never gets angry at the wicked, who does not feel repulsion but compassion for evil and twisted souls, that person is living according to the mind of Christ.

At least we who don't want to be Christians in name only, who aspire to true perfection, should endeavor, under the Cross of Jesus, to raise our eyes toward Him, and, with Him, as He teaches us, to pardon willingly all injuries, to pray for our enemies, and to pay back evil with good.

Let us never doubt the love of Jesus. This love remains faithful, even for the sheep who go astray.

6

Religious Obedience

God's will is observed in a sure fashion in obedience.

Remain obedient, trusting and sincere: you will become a saint.

The person who obeys down to the smallest details has sacrificed his will to God's.

Never forget that the person who obeys is walking in God's paths.

Obedience will save you. Obedience will lead you to holiness.

Obedience is in God's way, and in God's way is found God's blessing, and God's blessing is joy and peace.

Put obedience "to the test": your ship will not sink.

Obedience is the path of love.

Obedience is always love's guardian and its counselor.

Obedience will be your repose, but also your trial: your consolation and your cross.

The best penance is obedience and love.

Obey: because obedience is the first disciple of humility, and humility is the fruit of faith.

To be perfect is to accomplish God's will, and this is manifested in the express will of Superiors.

Religious Obedience

To be "less perfect" through obedience is more perfect than to tend to a "higher" perfection apart from obedience.

The devil doesn't fear penances, but obedience.

7

Poverty

The world is sick; with all its riches, this world is decaying and going into the abyss. It is sliding down a deadly slope and suffocating in its luxury. It is poverty that will heal it: poor priests will recover it and will bring it back to life. But I mean *poor*, poor like St. Francis of Assisi....

The evangelical life and the poverty of Jesus should shine so brightly in us that men recognize Him and love Him in us. People are still sensitive to a mortified sacerdotal life.

May all riches and all luxury be only weariness and grief to you. May all privations be your food, in the thought that they are the same food that Jesus, Mary, and Joseph consumed eagerly during their whole life.

Poverty is painful to the body, but it is treasure when it is endured for God.

8
Ascesis, *Mortification*, & *Self-offering*

At the altar, continue to sacrifice, through the simple and filial offering of each day, each action, each cross! Through the complete and fearless abandonment of our whole poor life to Jesus and Mary!

In every mortification, every offering of the day, we should give *ourselves*. In every grief, in every cross, love should lead us to the oblation of ourselves.

Apart from this work of continual immolation, our prayer and our spiritual conversations are nothing but superficial prattle and our sermons are words thrown to the wind.

Great souls live in recollection, energy, and fidelity in the smallest things. Great souls will not retreat when they face the complete sacrifice.

To offer yourself is to love: it is love without sentiment, love without sweetness; a pure love which lives by naked faith.

Prayer is necessary, but mortification and self-offering are worth still more.

Prayer is much, but sacrificing yourself is everything.

The most powerful, the most genuine prayer is the gift of self: remain a victim with the Victim, *hostia pro Hostia*.

Work is much, prayer is more, and self-offering and suffering are everything.

Ascesis, *Mortification, & Self-offering*

A sacrificed soul can never lose its calm or surrender its peace. It must always love God's will, even when all plans and hopes are ruined.

A sacrificed soul is a scrap, a little nothing: no one pays attention to it, no one values it, no one makes room for it. A victim soul is a thing under the feet of all, and also under the feet of Jesus.

Do not choose! A sacrificed soul must wait for everything and let Jesus direct.

Let us courageously embrace penance, yes, courageously, until we feel the sting. Only then will we experience the sweetness.

An offering is not preserved in sugar, but... in brine, in the biting salt of the brine.

UNDER THE GAZE OF GOD

Beware of this dangerous phrase: "I wish." Alas! We can repeat it until our deathbed and meanwhile drag along our lazy or irascible character through our whole life.

Only a mortified heart is free.

Faults are like weeds; it is useless to cut them, we must tear them out with the roots or they will come up again the next day.

The person who wants to eradicate all his faults at once will succeed in a few things and then will soon be discouraged.

Attack your faults one by one, cultivate one virtue after another, and your progress will be amazing.

As long as we do not apply ourselves to taking one point after another and doing the object of our examination of conscience, we will not be doing serious work.

Ascesis, Mortification, & Self-offering

Each victory over ourselves, each word, each unkind smile repressed is gold, precious gold.

The person who never hides the truth out of fear of displeasing others shows that he is detached from people.

The person who can be silent regarding another's faults has already finished one stage on the journey to perfection.

Being silent is costly, but precious for formation and perfection. No excuses, just be silent.

Being silent about someone is easy; but it becomes close to impossible to do it regarding a person about whom you have already complained to others.

UNDER THE GAZE OF GOD

Mortification in a soul who doesn't keep it hidden is water in a bucket which leaks: all it merits and good effects escape.

Let your defense, your personal apologetic, be silence full of Jesus's love.

Tell your difficulties to Jesus, to Mary, and your director. Apart from that, no one else.

Love and obedience give the value to mortification.

Humility, obedience, and love make mortification pleasing to God and to ourselves; it's like the sauce on a dish.

With regard to mortification keep only the love, obedience, and constancy which constitutes its great value. Our penances aren't small when they have these three qualities.

9
Humility

Let us repeat often before God that we are "nothing." Then he will make us see we can do "everything" in Him.

To seek to "appear" is to make Jesus "disappear."

Remain little in the eyes of others: use your knowledge, your abilities, but don't point them out, not even by words of false humility.

Never pose! To pose is wanting to attract attention to someone other than Jesus.

One does not become a great man unless one does not seek it: for seeking it is vanity and vanity is petty.

UNDER THE GAZE OF GOD

Be humble and take care that you don't let your humility be seen.

Don't think about the good you have done, but about the good you are still failing to do.

In order to be silent about ourselves, about the good as about the bad, we must be deeply mortified.

I don't know if it is good to reject praise or to speak ill of yourself. Whichever it is, I do not like it. A look at God's infinite mercy is humbler and safer than a refusal of praise.

Like being regarded as nothing. Then you will have peace.

Dishcloths are useful; lace handkerchiefs are only for looks.

Humility

The person who is not a wretch in his own eyes still isn't very far on the path of perfection.

Be simple and humble. Jesus loves those who are little.

The little and the poor are always welcome at Jesus's side.

The simple—the people who don't think about themselves—have entry into the Heart of Jesus.

How much we lose by not remaining children!

Pearls shine more against a dark background. Love to be little and forgotten.

Only those who are little do great things.

To humble yourself meekly before Jesus and Mary is the way to come out of dryness. Even after a fault or a long negligence, the quickest remedy is to kneel before God in humble trust.

Let us be "children" through simplicity and freedom. This costs something. It's a complete break with many little habits and innocent pleasures. It's truly a new life.... No, it's a true death!

Oh dearest Mother, obtain for me from your Jesus true simplicity, without which it is not possible to do any good. And may this simplicity consist above all in uprightness of intention.

We become humble only through humiliation. We become holy only through trials and darkness.

Humility

Only the humble, those who expect everything from God and Mary, will be able to persevere and do much good.

Patience is the express train for humility. And humility is the nearest station to perfection.

There is nothing to do but accept a humiliation: this immediately brings Jesus so near!

The one who is not surprised by his weakness in on the path of true humility.

Half of perfection is our ability to recognize our profound unworthiness and inability to do good.

Sometimes I rejoice to fall so often still and to see so much unfaithfulness in myself. Without that, how could I know myself and understand the *De Profundis*?

Holy Scripture is only clear for the weakness which has learned to know and admit itself.

In God's plan our weaknesses serve to give us knowledge of ourselves and dispose us to a great confidence in Him alone.

10

Love of the Cross & Trials

May the cross be for me like a kiss from the Crucified.

Suffer like Jesus: not for yourself alone, but for souls.

A cross loses half of its weight as soon as it is fully accepted.

What crucifies can become salvific: you can rejoice in it and give thanks for it, if you are able. And don't consider much what sort of wood crosses are made. They will always be made of "the wood of the Cross."

When you don't find God in your reflections and meditations, this path is still open to you: find God in your state in life, in your crosses, in the work imposed on you. All that is the envelope of God's will... and God's will is God Himself.

Love to be considered the least of all, and seek God in the cross.

A cross is a cross, but it's in the cross that Love allows itself to be found.

God has two ways of guiding souls: priests and crosses.

We must suffer, since without suffering and renunciation, we all go to our ruin.

The vocation of all the elect, of all religious—isn't it suffering and sacrifice? Therefore, isn't the cross the guide book for perfection?

A Christian without a cross is a soldier without his insignia.

Love of the Cross & Trials

Battles and crosses, all these cooperate with those who want to be sanctified.

Here below perfection consists in the love of suffering and the love of the cross.

Each one has his burden, each one has his cross. God has willed that each pay for his happiness with his cross; the intellectual by crucifying his intellect with humility and modesty; the mother in crucifying her heart through surrender and resignation; all through faith and love.

The ideal is the same for everyone, only the ways are different. What they all have in common is that they are ways of the cross: suffering through love, self-offering through love.

It's beautiful to see how all men are drawn to Him through suffering and trials, and how those whom He loves the most ascend the sorrowful Mount of Calvary of interior pain.

How many wish for perfection but fear the means to attain it! I don't know of a better way than the cross, especially interior crosses.

We will be sanctified in the measure that we suffer and love suffering.

If you are faithful to the cross, you soon will find a deep consolation in your cross itself.

If you do not fear the cross, you will go far and you will be happy.

Oh! Let us not fear the cross, the token of love, but embrace it willingly and carry it for Love. Let us ask for this in our prayers, so we can teach it to many others.

Love of the Cross & Trials

Let us embrace the cross: then it becomes sweet and sanctifying.

Never look at the cross (the trial) except to press it to your heart.

I live neither for my repose nor for my peace. I live for the cross and God's glory.

Be content with everything God sends you, and never wish to be freed from it, except insofar as He Himself wills it.

Don't observe what sort of wood your cross is made of; don't consider the one who places it on your shoulders; don't seek to see if it happened rightly or wrongly: such thoughts deprive the trial of its merits and remove its sweetness.

May every cross, interior or exterior, be a sign for you of imminent help and benediction.

Illness and interior dryness are sometimes more sanctifying than health and consolation.

Illnesses are pearls for the world, precious pearls — alas! — everywhere little valued.

If God crucifies and humbles you, this has much more worth than the most excellent mission.

Love makes us accept the cross and renders it light.

Love gives the cross value and merit.

What must we suffer? Everything divine Providence allows to happen to us: in ourselves, in our families, in our social life.

By bearing the little crosses of each day you will soon arrive at the love of the cross.

Great crosses are given rarely; little crosses are given to us at every hour. Watch, so that you don't lose any of them.

The grains of wheat for the little daily host, these are the tiresome duties of your state in life. A calm and consistent smile throughout a burdensome and wearying day, that is better grain. Being kind to everyone in the house and smiling amiably, that is the finest wheat.

How far we are from the example of the Savior when each of us esteems and loves ourselves and we have nothing to suffer! We resemble Jesus then the way a nettle resembles a rose.

Life is something different from playing marbles.

UNDER THE GAZE OF GOD

Remain above the wind, above what people say: God alone. Don't complain about your cross: it is the fertilizer for the field.

Love those who wound you through blame or insult: they are God's envoys.

There are no helps more precious to your work than those who destroy, hinder, and oppose it.

Differences of character are a cross more meritorious than the hair shirt and the discipline. It's a cross ordained by Providence; these sanctify us much more surely than all the crosses we would choose.

Never give in to sadness! It is extremely harmful to the soul. Accept and love! Shedding tears is not committing a fault if it isn't too frequent and doesn't leave you depressed.

Love of the Cross & Trials

Do not be distracted about vague pains without a definite object; it is enough to cast them into love as fuel for the fire: they don't indicate any blame on God's part.

Suffer from your failings but always with love's serene sweetness. Endure them for Jesus and not for yourself.

Suffer! Be silent! And always keep your good humor, even when everything in your soul is dark and black and the air is heavy with storms.

One profanes crosses the moment they are drawn from silence: they lose their savor and their strength.

Don't let your faith decay at the moment when God is sending you the most useful and most difficult lessons of your life.

UNDER THE GAZE OF GOD

God does not send us any cross which surpasses our powers: the powers which you lack now you will obtain through prayer.

A day will come when your sufferings will be changed into joy.

A day will come when with rapture you will thank God for his crosses.

I will not stop praying for you until the day I know you to be more happy with a cross than a success; the day on which you find more consolation in humiliations than in praise.

11

Prayer & Meditation

To have both recollection and good humor is a sign of the interior life.

Only the person who can find his consolation in God alone is secure.

To acquire the habit of recollection we must think in God's presence and speak to Him frequently.

Converse more with Jesus than with men.

Speak with less noise and less gesticulation. Remain under the gaze of God everywhere.

You learn more at the feet of Jesus and Mary than by the most strenuous human efforts.

Seek your consolation with Jesus, since the words of men do not satisfy the heart.

Don't grumble about your lack of spiritual progress, about dryness, or persistent darkness: that is not generosity but ego.

Spiritual aridity is a beneficial atmosphere.

The more difficult and painful prayers are and the more effort they cost the heart, the more meritorious they are in God's eyes.

Our little perverse "I" falls so easily into pride when Jesus lets the honey flow: vinegar and gall are a better diet for it.

Continue to make your interior prayer as before: your aversions, your difficulties, your dryness do not prevent you. Let this be the prayer of consent, the prayer of *"fiat."* Sometimes it consists only in staying there suffering before Jesus and Mary: "Jesus the one whom you love is sick." That is enough. And it is not time wasted.

We can seem dry, but we will never be empty as long as we have desire. Desire is the lover's currency, however weak he feels himself to be.

When you experience interior darkness and you can't pray, you can count on greater graces for your work.

Whatever your prayers may be, sweet and happy or sad and dry, they are always pleasing to God from the moment your will is in accord with His.

Pray the whole day, through the loving fulfillment of your hundred little duties of state.

Let your day be a firework of little burning aspirations.

UNDER THE GAZE OF GOD

One peaceful thanksgiving after Communion nourishes the soul more than agitation in the desires and exercises of piety. Peace is a permanent homage of trust and faith.

Prayer and Communion give you the fuel to burn; it's for you to make a fire with them, otherwise you will die of cold beside the coals.

Never do your spiritual reading with haste and agitation. Don't read too much because that would remove the unction and fruitfulness from it.

What good does it do you to hear the best and most beautiful things if you take nothing away from them or do not make use of them in your life?

When you go into a shop, it's for the purpose of buying. It's not enough to examine the merchandise: you must bring away something. That is what you should do at each spiritual instruction, so you can say, "Here is something for me, I will keep this!"

Don't lose the grace, open it. There are graces which don't return.

Each meditation, each spiritual reading which we subtract from our interior life is a stone we remove from the foundations of our priestly life. This building can also preserve a lovely façade at the same time, but soon fissures form in the walls, and it collapses. Who would have guessed it?

Frequently make an hour of prayer: an hour as a victim, an hour of desire, an hour of contemplation, or even an hour of patience, but always with Mary.

In prayer we look at God, we take his thoughts into ourselves, we incorporate his perfections into ourselves. We are illumined by His love, repaired by his grace, and configured to him.

To live in the Sacred Heart of Jesus is to comprehend His Heart and to be intimately and totally seized by Him.

Our heaven begins on earth when we have found Jesus in our soul.

A drop of mysticism sometimes does more than a pound of asceticism.

A truly spiritual person lives with the awareness of his littleness and powerlessness. His love grows through the awareness of his faults. He loves to be forgotten; if he comes to be known, he forgets himself, for Him!

Don't talk about your spiritual life: that makes it evaporate.

The true mystic never loses the conviction that she is poor in herself and that in the depth which is her own being, she is a very miserable little nothing.

"Libenter gloriabor!" Gladly will I rejoice in my weaknesses! This is the food of the mystical soul in her littleness.

12

The Apostolate

The apostolate is a life consistent with the truth.

In our exterior apostolate we must give the primacy to interior action. In these matters, the truth is revenged each time we lose sight of the principles.

Frequently we lose the trail of the supernatural when we expect too much from a fury of activity.

We should ceaselessly bring the faithful to acquire a more lively faith and a more supernatural understanding: this is the most certain means of ensuring the success of our apostolic enterprises.

All the means of the apostolate should converge towards this great means: *"fides in gratia"* (the faith in grace), which we should cause to be respected, to conquer, and to be maintained.

After the Mass, our great apostolate is to fill ourselves with *His* Spirit and *His* love.

In order to write about Him and about her in a fervent and profound way, in calm and recollection, we should grow with Him and her; our spiritual life must govern our apostolate.

Prayer, faith, and penance are the great pedagogical forces.

Put Christ in your place in all your exercises, desires, and efforts. This is the correct order: it is what Mary did.

The Apostolate

If we look to the omnipotence of Jesus when we speak, our words become full of *His* unction and *His* power.

Fine words, holy sayings, all these count for so little! The grace of God, the action of God in our soul, our prayer—that is everything!

Holy words don't nourish if they are inwardly empty.

What a difference there is between one word from a saint and a whole discourse from a pretentious person!

Only flame starts a fire.

Dip your pen in the incandescent flame of the Holy Spirit.

The heart of a priest which does not bleed is not the heart of a priest.

UNDER THE GAZE OF GOD

No one is more certain of his salvation than a priest who is fulfilling his duties.

The future is in the hands of God; God places it in the hands of priests.

Let us sow, let us sow ceaselessly! May our motto be, "Sow!" Something from it will always stay in the life of our little ones, in any case enough for their last hour. Every objection falls before this primary consideration.

"Always sow": your motto. If this is in tears, so much the better. That will water the words and the "Sun" will then ripen the crop.

The world isn't interested in "good men." It's only the holy, the humble, the penitent whom they still consent to listen to. But it's time!... They no longer believe our words, but they will believe our actions.

The Apostolate

Remember Your sufferings, Jesus. Remember Your love, and the innocence of the little ones! Send us Your priests!

A Prayer for Blessed Edward Poppe's Canonization

Our Father who art in heaven, we praise you because you have given us Blessed Father Poppe.

May he, with you, remain near us at this time when we have such need of saints and witnesses to your life and your love.

May he teach us to do your will, and always, in joy and in suffering, count on your mercy.

May we, like him, learn to love Jesus without measure, in His word and in the Eucharist.

May we always follow the inspirations of your Spirit in prayer and in all the circumstances of life.

May we, like him, love the pilgrim Church.
May his canonization give the Church in the new millennium a powerful impulse toward a great concern for the poor and the little ones, for the formation given to priests and teachers needed in schools, parishes, and families, for understanding the signs of the times, and for evangelizing the world.
Father of mercies, we ask you urgently to show us the way to your Son, in the company of our holy Mother Mary, whom Blessed Father Poppe loved so much.

Our Father.
Hail Mary.
Glory Be.

Blessed Edward Poppe, pray for us.